# Table of Contents

Introduction .................................................................. 2
    Multiple Sclerosis (MS) ........................................... 3
    Symptoms Of MS .................................................... 3
    Types Of Multiple Sclerosis ..................................... 8
    Causes of Multiple Sclerosis (MS) ............................ 13
    Triggers Of MS Symptoms ...................................... 18
    Testing & Research ................................................ 20
    Diagnostic criteria .................................................. 25
    Multiple Sclerosis (MS) Treatments ......................... 26
    Medications for physical symptoms ........................ 30
Living With MS ............................................................ 35
    Medications .......................................................... 35
    MS and Diet .......................................................... 36
    Effects Of MS ........................................................ 41
    Prognosis For People With MS ................................ 42
    MS type ................................................................ 43
Natural Remedies And MS ............................................ 43
    Chinese Herbs For MS ........................................... 45
    Supplements For MS ............................................. 66
    DHA ...................................................................... 68
    Multimineral and multivitamin supplements .......... 71

## Introduction

Although no drug or supplement can cure Multiple sclerosis (MS), some treatments may help people slow the disease's progress. Other therapies can significantly reduce symptoms or prolong periods of remission. Around the world, people with MS use complementary and alternative medicine. Many people turn to nonpharmaceutical treatments when Western medicine doesn't work to improve their symptoms. Others decide to try these options when their healthcare provider makes a referral or when they hear about the promise of alternative treatments. Regardless of your reasons for seeking information on herbal and supplementary treatments for MS, always consult your healthcare provider before stopping prescribed medications or adding a new therapy to your treatment regimen. Although no drug or supplement can cure MS, some treatments may help people slow the disease's progress. Other therapies can significantly reduce symptoms or prolong periods of remission. Around the world, people with MS use complementary and alternative medicine. Many people turn to nonpharmaceutical treatments when Western medicine doesn't work to improve their symptoms. Others decide to try these options when their healthcare provider makes a referral or when they hear about the promise of alternative treatments. Regardless of your reasons for seeking information on herbal and supplementary treatments for MS, always consult your healthcare provider before stopping prescribed medications or adding a new therapy to your treatment regimen.

## Multiple Sclerosis (MS)

Multiple sclerosis (MS) is a chronic illness involving your central nervous system (CNS). The immune system attacks myelin, which is the protective layer around nerve fibers. This causes inflammation and scar tissue, or lesions. This can make it hard for your brain to send signals to the rest of your body.

## Symptoms Of MS

Multiple sclerosis (MS) is a progressive, immune-mediated disorder. That means the system designed to keep your body healthy mistakenly attacks parts of your body that are vital to everyday function. The protective coverings of nerve cells are damaged, which leads to diminished function in the brain and spinal cord. MS is a disease with unpredictable symptoms that can vary in intensity. While some people experience fatigue and numbness, severe cases of MS can cause paralysis, vision loss, and diminished brain function. Common early signs of multiple sclerosis (MS) include:

- vision problems

- tingling and numbness

- pains and spasms

- weakness or fatigue

- balance problems or dizziness

- bladder issues

- sexual dysfunction

- cognitive problems

Vision problems

Visual problems are one of the most common symptoms of MS. Inflammation affects the optic nerve and disrupts central vision. This can cause blurred vision, double vision, or loss of vision. You may not notice the vision problems immediately, as degeneration of clear vision can be slow. Pain when you look up or to one side also can accompany vision loss. There are variety of ways to cope with MS-related vision changes.

Tingling and numbness

MS affects nerves in the brain and spinal cord (the body's message center). This means it can send conflicting signals around the body. Sometimes, no signals are sent. This results in numbness. Tingling sensations and numbness are one of the most common warning signs of MS. Common sites of numbness include the face, arms, legs, and fingers.

Pain and spasms

Chronic pain and involuntary muscle spasmsare also common with MS. One study, according to the National MS Society, showed that half of people with MS had chronic pain. Muscle stiffness or spasms (spasticity) are also common. You might experience stiff muscles or joints as well as uncontrollable, painful jerking movements of the extremities. The legs are most often affected, but back pain is also common.

Fatigue and weakness

Unexplained fatigue and weakness affect about 80 percent of people in the early stages of MS. Chronic fatigue occurs when nerves deteriorate in the spinal column. Usually, the fatigue appears suddenly and lasts for weeks before improving. The weakness is most noticeable in the legs at first.

Balance problems and dizziness

Dizziness and problems with coordination and balance can decrease the mobility of someone with MS. Your doctor may refer to these as problems with your gait. People with MS often feel lightheaded, dizzy, or as if their surroundings are spinning (vertigo). This symptom often occurs when you stand up.

Bladder and bowel dysfunction

A dysfunctional bladder is another symptom occurring in up to 80 percent of people with MS. This can include frequent urination, strong urges to urinate, or inability to hold in urine. Urinary-related symptoms are often manageable. Less often, people with MS experience constipation, diarrhea, or loss of bowel control.

Sexual dysfunction

Sexual arousal can also be a problem for people with MS because it begins in the central nervous system — where MS attacks.

Cognitive problems

About half of people with MS will develop some kind of issue with their cognitive function. This can include:

• memory problems

• shortened attention span

• language problems

• difficulty staying organized

Depression and other emotional health problems are also common.

Changes in emotional health

Major depression is common among people with MS. The stresses of MS can also cause irritability, mood swings, and a condition called pseudobulbar affect. This involves bouts of uncontrollable crying and laughing. Coping with MS symptoms, along with relationship or family issues, can make depression and other emotional disorders even more challenging.

**Other symptoms**

Not everyone with MS will have the same symptoms. Different symptoms can manifest during relapses or attacks. Along with the symptoms mentioned on the previous slides, MS can also cause:

• hearing loss

• seizures

• uncontrollable shaking

• breathing problems

• slurred speech

• trouble swallowing

## Types Of Multiple Sclerosis

Multiple sclerosis (MS) is thought to be an autoimmune, inflammatory disease affecting the central nervous system and peripheral nerves. The cause remains unknown, but some studies indicate a link between the Epstein Barr Virus, while others indicate environmental factors, a lack of vitamin D, or parasites as a stimulus of the persistent immune response in the central nervous system. It can be unpredictable and, in some cases, disabling. But not all forms of MS are the same. To help distinguish between the different types of the condition, the National Multiple Sclerosis Society (NMSS) identified four distinct categories. To accurately define the different forms of MS, in 1996, the NMSS surveyed a group of scientists who specialized in MS patient care and research. After analyzing the scientists' responses, the organization categorized the condition into four primary types. These course definitions were updated in 2013 to reflect advances in research. They are:

• clinically isolated syndrome (CIS)

• relapsing-remitting MS (RRMS)

• primary-progressive MS (PPMS)

• secondary-progressive MS (SPMS)

The four categories defined by the NMSS are now relied upon by the medical community at large and create a common language for diagnosing and treating MS. The categories' classifications are based on how far the disease has progressed in each patient.

Clinically isolated syndrome

Clinically isolated syndrome (CIS) is a single episode of neurologic symptoms that lasts 24 hours or more. Your symptoms cannot be tied to fever, infection, or other illness. They're the result of inflammation or demyelination in the central nervous system. You might have only one symptom (monofocal episode) or several (multifocal episode). If you have CIS, you may never experience another episode. Or this episode could be your first MS attack. If an MRI detects brain lesions similar to those found in people with MS, there's a 60 to 80 percent chance you'll have another episode and a diagnosis of MS within a few years. At this time, you might have a diagnosis of MS if an MRI detects older lesions in a different part of your central nervous system. That would mean you've had a previous attack, even if you weren't aware of it.

Relapsing-remitting MS

The most common type is relapsing-remitting MS (RRMS). According to the NMSS, approximately 85 percent of people with MS have this type at the time of diagnosis. When you have RRMS you may experience:

• clearly defined relapses or flare-ups that result in episodes of intensive worsening of your neurologic function

• partial or complete remissions or recovery periods after the relapses and between attacks when the disease stops progressing

• mild to severe symptoms as well as relapses and remissions that last for days or months

Progressive types of MS

While the vast majority of people with MS have the RRMS form, some are diagnosed with a progressive form of the disease: primary-progressive MS (PPMS) or secondary-progressive MS (SPMS). Each of these types indicates that the disease continues to worsen without improvement.

Primary-progressive MS

This form of MS progresses slowly yet steadily from the time of its onset. Symptoms stay at the same level of intensity without decreasing, and there are no remission periods. In essence, patients with PPMS experience a fairly continuous worsening of their condition. However, there can be variations in the rate of progression over the course of the disease — as well as the possibility of minor improvements (usually temporary) and occasional plateaus in symptom progression. The NMSS estimates that approximately 15 percent of people with MS have PPMS at the onset of the condition.

Secondary-progressive MS

SPMS is more of a mixed bag. Initially, it may involve a period of relapsing-remitting activity, with symptom flare-ups followed by recovery periods. Yet the disability of MS doesn't disappear between cycles. Instead, this period of fluctuation is followed by a steady worsening of the condition. People with SPMS may experience minor remissions or plateaus in their symptoms, but this isn't always the case. Without treatment, about half of people with RRMS go on to develop SPMS within a decade.

Type casting

Early MS can be challenging for doctors to diagnose. As such, it can be helpful to understand the characteristics and symptoms of MS at the time of initial diagnosis —

particularly since the vast majority of people with the disease exhibit characteristics of relapsing-remitting MS. Although MS currently has no cure, it isn't normally fatal. In fact, most people who have MS never become severely disabled, according to the NMSS. Identifying MS early at the relapsing-remitting stage can help ensure prompt treatment to avoid developing more progressive forms of the illness.

## Causes of Multiple Sclerosis (MS)

Multiple sclerosis (MS) is a progressive neurological disease that can affect the central nervous system (CNS). Every time you take a step, blink, or move your arm, your CNS is at work. Millions of nerve cells in the brain send signals throughout the body to control these processes and functions:

• movement

• sensation

• memory

• cognition

• speech

Nerve cells communicate by sending electrical signals via nerve fibers. A layer called the myelin sheath covers and protects these fibers. That protection ensures that each nerve cell properly reaches its intended target. In people with MS, immune cells mistakenly attack and damage the myelin sheath. This damage results in the disruption of nerve signals. Damaged nerve signals can cause debilitating symptoms, including:

• walking and coordination problems

• muscle weakness

• fatigue

• vision problems

MS affects everyone differently. The severity of the disease and the types of symptoms vary from person to person. There are different types of MS, and the cause, symptoms, progression of disability may vary. The exact cause of MS is unknown. However, scientists believe that four factors may play a role in the development of the disease.

Cause 1: Immune system

MS is considered an immune-mediated disease: The immune system malfunctions and attacks the CNS. Researchers know that the myelin sheath is directly affected, but they don't know what triggers the immune system to attack the myelin. Research into which immune cells are responsible for the attack is ongoing. Scientists are seeking to uncover what causes these cells to attack. They're also searching for methods to control or stop the progression of the disease.

Cause 2: Genetics

Several genes are believed to play a role in MS. Your chance of developing MS is slightly higher if a close relative, such as a parent or sibling, has the disease. According to the National Multiple Sclerosis Society, if one parent or sibling has MS, the chances of getting the disease are estimated to be around 2.5 to 5 percent in the United States. The chances for an average person are approximately 0.1 percent. Scientists believe that people with MS are born with a genetic susceptibility to react to certain unknown environmental agents. An autoimmune response is triggered when they encounter these agents.

Cause 3: Environment

Epidemiologists have seen an increased pattern of MS cases in countries located farthest from the equator. This correlation causes some to believe that vitamin D may play a role. Vitamin D benefits immune system function. People who live near the equator are exposed to more sunlight. As a result, their bodies produce more vitamin D. The longer your skin is exposed to sunlight, the more your body naturally produces the vitamin. Since MS is considered an immune-mediated disease, vitamin D and sunlight exposure may be linked to it.

Cause 4: Infection

Researchers are considering the possibility that bacteria and viruses may cause MS. Viruses are known to cause inflammation and a breakdown of myelin. Therefore, it's possible that a virus could trigger MS. It's also possible that the bacteria or virus that have similar components to brain cells trigger the immune system to mistakenly identify normal brain cells as foreign and destroy them. Several bacteria and viruses are being investigated to determine if they contribute to the development of MS. These include:

- measles viruses

- human herpes virus-6, which leads to conditions such as roseola

- Epstein-Barr virus

Other risk factors

Other risk factors may also increase your chances of developing MS. These include:

- Sex. Women are at least two to three times more likely to develop relapsing-remitting multiple sclerosis (RRMS) than men. In the primary-progressive (PPMS) form, numbers of men and women are approximately equal.

- Age. RRMS usually affects people between the ages of 20 and 50. PPMS usually occurs approximately 10 years later than other forms.

- Ethnicity. People of northern European descent are at highest risk of developing MS

## Triggers Of MS Symptoms

There are several triggers that people with MS should avoid.

### Stress

Stress can trigger and worsen MS symptoms. Practices that help you reduce and cope with stress can be beneficial. Add de-stressing rituals to your day, such as yoga or meditation.

### Smoking

Cigarette smoke can add to the progression of MS. If you smoke, look into effective methods of quitting. Avoid being around secondhand smoke.

### Heat

Not everyone sees a difference in symptoms due to heat, but avoid direct sun or hot tubs if you find you react to them.

### Medication

There are several ways that medication can worsen symptoms. If you're taking many drugs and they interact poorly, talk to your doctor. They can decide which drugs are vital and which ones you may be able to stop taking.

Some people stop taking their MS medications because they have too many side effects or they believe they aren't effective. However, these medicines are critical to help prevent relapses and new lesions, so it's important to stay on them.

Lack of sleep

Fatigue is a common symptom of MS. If you're not getting enough sleep, this can decrease your energy even more.

Infections

From urinary tract infections to the cold or flu, infections can cause your symptoms to worsen. In fact, infections cause approximately one-third of all flare-ups of MS symptoms, according to the Cleveland Clinic.

Tests For Multiple Sclerosis

Multiple sclerosis can be difficult to diagnosis; there is no single test that can diagnose it. Instead, a diagnosis typically requires multiple tests to rule out other conditions with similar symptoms. After your doctor conducts a physical examination, they'll likely order several different tests if they suspect you may have MS.

Blood tests

Blood tests will likely be part of the initial workup if your doctor suspects you might have MS. Blood tests can't currently result in a firm diagnosis of MS, but they can rule out other conditions. These conditions include:

• Lyme disease

• rare hereditary disorders

• syphilis

• HIV/AIDS

All of these disorders can be diagnosed with bloodwork alone. Blood tests can also reveal abnormal results. This can lead toward diagnoses such as cancer or a vitamin B-12 deficiency.

## Testing & Research
Magnetic resonance imaging

Magnetic resonance imaging (MRI) is the test of choice for diagnosing MS in combination with initial blood tests. MRIs use radio waves and magnetic fields to evaluate the relative water content in tissues of the body. They can detect normal and abnormal tissues and can spot irregularities. MRIs offer detailed and sensitive images of the brain and spinal cord. They're much less invasive than X-rays or CT scans, which both use radiation.

Purpose: Doctors will be looking for two things when they order an MRI with a suspected diagnosis of MS. The first is that they'll check for any other abnormalities that could rule out MS and point to a different diagnosis, such as a brain tumor. They'll also look for evidence of demyelination. The layer of myelin that protects the nerve fibers is fatty and repels water when it's undamaged. If the myelin has been damaged, however, this fat content is reduced or stripped away entirely and no longer repels water. The area will hold more water as a result, which can be detected by MRIs. To diagnose MS, doctors must find evidence of demyelination. In addition to ruling out other potential conditions, an MRI can provide solid evidence that demyelination has occurred.

Preparation: Before you go in for your MRI, remove all jewelry. If you have any metal on your clothes (including zippers or bra hooks), you'll be asked to change into a hospital gown. You'll lie still inside the MRI machine (which is open on both ends) for the duration of the procedure, which takes between 45 minutes and 1 hour. Let your doctor and technician know ahead of time if you have:

- metallic implants
- pacemaker
- tattoos
- implanted drug infusions
- artificial heart valves
- history of diabetes
- any other conditions that you think could be relevant

Lumbar puncture

Lumbar puncture, also called a spinal tap, is sometimes used in the process of diagnosing MS. This procedure will remove a sample of the cerebrospinal fluid (CSF) for testing. Lumbar punctures are considered invasive. During the procedure, a needle is inserted into the lower back, between vertebrae, and into the spinal canal. This hollow needle will collect the sample of CSF for testing. A spinal tap typically takes about 30 minutes, and you will be given a local anesthetic. The patient is typically asked to lay on their side with their spine curved. After the area has been cleaned and a local anesthetic has been administered, a doctor will inject the hollow needle into the spinal canal to withdraw one to two tablespoons of CSF. Usually, there is no special preparation. You may be asked to stop taking blood thinners. Doctors who order lumbar punctures during the process of an MS diagnosis will use the test to rule out conditions with similar symptoms. They'll also look for signs of MS, specifically:

• elevated levels of antibodies called IgG antibodies

• proteins called oligoclonal bands

• an unusually high amount of white blood cells

The number of white blood cells in the spinal fluid of people with MS can be up to seven times higher than normal. However, these abnormal immune responses can also be caused by other conditions. It's also estimated that 5 to 10 percent of people with MS do not show any abnormalities in their CSF.

Evoked potential test

Evoked potential (EP) tests measure the electrical activity in the brain that occurs in response to stimulation, such as sound, touch, or sight. Each type of stimuli evokes minute electrical signals, which can be measured by the electrodes placed on the scalp to monitor activity in certain areas of the brain. There are three types of EP tests. The visual evoked response (VER or VEP) is the one most commonly used to diagnose MS. When doctors order an EP test, they're going to look for impaired transmission that is present along the optic nerve pathways. This typically happens fairly early in most MS patients. However, before concluding that abnormal VERs are due to MS, other ocular or retinal disorders must be excluded. No preparation is necessary to take an EP test. During the test, you'll sit in front of a screen that has an alternating checkerboard pattern on it. You may be asked to cover one eye at a time. It does require active concentration, but it's safe and noninvasive. If you wear glasses, ask your doctor ahead of time if you should bring them.

New tests under development

Medical knowledge is always advancing. As technology and our knowledge of MS moves forward, doctors may find new tests to make the MS diagnosis process an easier one. A blood test is currently being developed that will be able to detect biomarkers that are associated with MS. While this test likely won't be able to diagnose MS on its own, it can help doctors evaluate risk factors and make diagnosis just a little easier.

## Diagnostic criteria

Doctors may have to repeat diagnostic tests for MS several times before they can confirm the diagnosis. This is because MS symptoms can change. They may diagnose someone with MS if testing points to the following criteria:

• Signs and symptoms indicate there's damage to the myelin in the CNS.

• The doctor has identified at least two or more lesions in two or more parts of the CNS via an MRI.

• There's evidence based on a physical exam that the CNS has been affected.

• A person has had two or more episodes of affected neurological function for at least one day, and they occurred a month apart. Or, a person's symptoms have progressed over the course of one year.

- The doctor can't find any other explanation for the person's symptoms.

Diagnostic criteria have changed over the years and will likely continue to change as new technology and research comes along. The most recent accepted criteria were published in 2017 as the revised McDonald Criteria. The International Panel on the Diagnosis of Multiple Sclerosis released these criteria. One of the more recent innovations in diagnosing MS is a tool called optical coherence tomography (OCT). This tool allows a doctor to obtain images of a person's optical nerve. The test is painless and is much like taking a picture of your eye. Doctors know that people with MS tend to have optic nerves that look different from people who don't have the disease. OCT also allows a doctor to track a person's eye health by looking at the optic nerve.

## Multiple Sclerosis (MS) Treatments

While there's no cure for multiple sclerosis (MS), there are many treatments available. These treatments mainly focus on slowing down the progression of the disease and managing symptoms. Different people can have different types of MS. And disease progression and symptoms range greatly from person to person. For both reasons, each person's treatment plan will be different.

Disease-modifying drugs

Disease-modifying medications can reduce the frequency and severity of MS episodes, or relapses. They also can control the growth of lesions (damage to nerve fibers) and reduce symptoms. There are currently several drugs approved by the Food and Drug Administration (FDA) for modifying MS. They come as injectables, infusions, and oral treatments.

Injectables: These four medications are given as injections:

• interferon beta-1a (Avonex, Rebif)

• interferon beta-1b (Betaseron, Extavia)

• glatiramer acetate (Copaxone, generic versions such as Glatopa)

• pegylated interferon beta-1a (Plegridy)

In 2018, the manufacturers of the injection daclizumab (Zinbryta) withdrew it from the market due to safety concerns.

Infusions: These four therapies must be given by infusion at a licensed clinic:

- alemtuzumab (Lemtrada)
- mitoxantrone (Novantrone)
- natalizumab (Tysabri)
- ocrelizumab (Ocrevus)

Oral treatments: These five treatments you take by mouth as pills:

- teriflunomide (Aubagio)
- fingolimod (Gilenya)
- dimethyl fumarate (Tecfidera)
- cladribine (Mavenclad)
- siponimod (Mayzent)

Treatments for relapses

Ending a relapse as quickly as possible benefits both the body and the mind. That's where relapse treatments come in.

Corticosteroids: Inflammation is a key feature of MS relapses. It can lead to many other symptoms of MS, such as:

• fatigue

• weakness

• pain

Corticosteroids are often used to ease inflammation and reduce the severity of MS attacks. Corticosteroids used to treat MS include methylprednisolone (intravenous) and prednisone (oral).

Other treatments: If corticosteroids don't provide relief for relapses, or if intravenous treatments can't be used, there are other treatments. These may include:

• ACTH (H.P. Acthar Gel): ACTH is an injection into your muscle or under your skin. It works by prompting the adrenal cortex gland to secrete the hormones cortisol, corticosterone, and aldosterone. These hormones reduce the level of inflammation in your body.

• Plasmapheresis: This processinvolves removing whole blood from your body and filtering it to remove antibodies that may be attacking your nervous system. The "cleansed" blood is then given back to you as a transfusion.

• Intravenous immunoglobulin (IVIG): This treatment is an injection that helps to boost your immune system. However, evidence of its benefits for MS relapses has been inconsistent in clinical studies.

### Medications for physical symptoms

While the drugs listed above help treat MS, a range of medications are available to treat the different physical symptoms that MS can cause.

Drugs for pain and other muscle problems: Muscle relaxants are often prescribed for people with MS. That's because relaxing muscles helps with common MS symptoms such as:

• pain

• muscle spasms

• fatigue

Relieving those symptoms can also help with depression, which can occur with MS. Drugs for muscle stiffness include:

- baclofen (Lioresal)

- cyclobenzaprine (Flexeril)

- diazepam (Valium)

- tizanidine (Zanaflex)

Drugs for fatigue: Fatigue is a common symptom for people with MS. Drugs used to treat fatigue include modafinil (Provigil). They also include amantadine hydrochloride (Gocovri), which is used off-label for this purpose. Off-label use is when a drug that's approved for one purpose is used for another. Fluoxetine (Prozac) is also often prescribed since it helps combat both fatigue and depression.

Drugs for bladder and bowel problems: There are more than a dozen prescription medications for bladder problems (such as incontinence) related to MS. Talk to your doctor about which drugs might be best for you. The most effective medications for constipation and bowel symptoms associated with MS seem to be over-the-counter stool softeners. If you have questions about these products, ask your pharmacist.

Exercise and physical therapy

Constant movement and activity are critical to fighting MS. Exercise helps:

- improve muscle strength

- increase cardiovascular health

- improve mood

- improve cognitive function

However, people with MS often experience fatigue. And when you're tired, you may not feel like exercising. But the less exercise you get, the more tired you'll feel. That's another reason why exercise, including physical therapy (PT), is so important. However, it needs to be carefully tailored to people with MS. Things such as keeping session times short and increasing exercise over time are important factors.

When to seek PT: Someone with MS should consider PT during a relapse that has produced a change in functions such as:

- walking

- coordination

- strength

- energy

The goal of PT during relapse is to return to a prior level of function, if possible.

Benefits of PT: A professional PT program will help improve your strength and physical function. It may also include self-care activities such as:

- home exercise programs

- aqua therapy

- yoga

- a personal fitness program at a gym or health club

Getting out of the house to exercise has the bonus of helping to address depression and social isolation that people with MS can experience.

Where to begin: A good way to start your MS exercise routine is to try basic stretches while you're sitting or in bed. When you feel comfortable with those exercises, add more demanding exercises such as walking, water exercise, or dancing. As you get stronger and more comfortable exercising, you can modify and build on your exercise program. Keep in mind that anything you can do with others, especially exercise you enjoy, can help.

Managing emotions during change

If you have MS, physical symptoms aren't the only things you have to deal with. You may face a constantly changing illness, which can make coping with your condition emotionally challenging. You might feel symptoms that include:

- depression

- grief

- emotional instability

- anger

Two popular treatment options are medication and therapy. But while antidepressants can often help relieve symptoms, they may not be enough. And although talk therapy with a licensed practitioner is a good idea, you may need help from someone who has a more personal understanding of MS. Your next step might be to find someone to talk to who understands what you're going through. Look to your local MS Society for education, counseling references, and support groups. Talking with people who know what it means to have MS can provide you with coping strategies and remind you that you're not the only one dealing with this condition.

## Living With MS

Most people with MS find ways to manage their symptoms and function well.

### Medications

Having MS means you'll need to see a doctor experienced in treating MS. If you take one of the DMTs, you'll have to make sure you adhere to the recommended schedule. Your doctor may prescribe other medications to treat specific symptoms.

Diet and exercise

A well-balanced diet, low in empty calories and high in nutrients and fiber, will help you manage your overall health. Regular exercise is important for physical and mental health, even if you have disabilities. If physical movement is difficult, swimming or exercising in a swimming pool can help. Some yoga classes are designed just for people with MS.

**Other complementary therapies**

Studies regarding the effectiveness of complementary therapies are scarce, but that doesn't mean they can't help in some way. The following may help you feel less stressed and more relaxed:

- meditation

- massage

- tai chi

- acupuncture

- hypnotherapy

- music therapy

## MS and Diet

If you have multiple sclerosis (MS), you've probably heard conflicting claims about a new diet or supplement that could help your symptoms. More studies are now being done to examine how nutrition can impact people living with MS. However, many results have been conflicting or inconclusive. Some diet plans can jeopardize your health and omit nutrients. So, eating a well-balanced, low-fat diet full of fiber and colorful fruits and vegetables is likely the best place to start. Talk with your doctor to find out the facts before starting any diet plan.

Low fat for good health

According to the National Multiple Sclerosis Society, many neurologists recommend a low-fat, high-fiber diet to maintain optimal health. This includes avoiding saturated fats and trans fats, and eating healthy mono- and polyunsaturated fats such as those found in olive oil, nuts, and avocados. Unsaturated fats are important building blocks of myelin and nervous system tissue. Keep in mind that moderation is the key. Less than 30 percent of daily calories should come from any kind of fat.

Swank diet has mixed results

In the 1980s, Dr. Roy Swank developed a very strict, low-fat diet for people with MS. In the Swank diet, fats are restricted. Fish oils are allowed. According to the Swank MS Foundation, overall calories from fat should be less than 30 percent of daily intake — a maximum of 65 grams of total fat per day. In a 1990 article in the Lancet, Swank's research group reported that people with MS who followed his diet saw less deterioration and lower mortality rates. However, some researchers aren't convinced there's enough current data to back up his claims. Studies are ongoing to determine if the Swank diet or other extremely low-fat diets have significant benefits for people with MS.

PUFA

Several studies have shown that increasing intake of polyunsaturated fatty acids (PUFAs) may help people with MS. These unsaturated fats have anti-inflammatory effects in animal studies. Linoleic acid, an omega-6 fatty acid, in combination with other nutrients including omega-3 fatty acids, decreased relapse rates and slowed disease progression in a clinical trial. However, other studies show no effect. Overall, researchers are not yet sure if it's worthwhile to add supplementation with PUFAs to an MS treatment regimen. Studies are inconclusive, and research is ongoing.

Vitamin D

Research published in the Journal of the Academy of Nutrition and Dietetics indicates that sufficient vitamin D levels may prevent the development of autoimmune diseases like MS. Research published in the Journal of Therapeutic Advances in Neurological Disorders suggests that vitamin D can also influence relapse rate and the number of lesions seen on MRIs. However, more studies are needed for conclusive evidence. Many neurologists recommend supplementation if blood levels are low. Recommended daily intake of vitamin D is 600 IU for adults (not to exceed 4000 IU per day). For patients with very low vitamin D levels, doctors may recommend taking more than that for a few months to bring vitamin D levels back to normal. However, too much vitamin D can be toxic, so it's important to speak with your doctor before taking any supplements.

Gluten

The effects of a gluten-free diet on MS are conflicting. Research from Israel suggests that some people with MS also have antibodies that are normally associated with celiac disease, a digestive disorder caused by an abnormal immune reaction to gluten. Gluten is a protein found in wheat and some other grains. The presence of these antibodies suggests a link between immune intolerance to gluten and autoimmune diseases like MS. However, other research findings and some neurologists suggest that there is no link between gluten antibodies and MS. More studies need to be done to draw any solid conclusions.

Antioxidants

Free radicals do some of the damage that occurs during the formation of MS lesions. Free radicals cause oxidative stress, and can be neutralized by antioxidants like vitamins A, C, E, beta carotene, lutein, lycopene, and selenium. A study in 2015 revealed that people with MS had significantly lower antioxidant levels and higher oxidative stress in their saliva. Chronic inflammation during an attack can cause deficiencies in antioxidant levels in the body. Supplementation may restore levels of these key nutrients. However, high doses may have other effects, not yet been studied on people with MS.

Ongoing research

Researchers are looking into the role that nutrition can play in treating MS, but many questions remain. Vitamin D shows promise in slowing the progression of MS. Omega-3 and omega-6 fatty acids may be valuable in protecting nerve health. Antioxidants and other nutrients like probiotics may also play valuable roles in a treatment regimen. How the gut microbiome (intestinal bacteria population) affects neurodegenerative diseases is a new frontier in research. Early research shows that improving gut bacteria can reduce the risk of gut permeability. It may also improve symptoms of MS and slow the progression of the disease. For now, a diet low in fat, high in fiber, and rich in plant foods — fruits, vegetables, and whole grains — seems to be the most evidence-based diet for the best long-term health of a person living with MS. However, there's not enough evidence yet to show clear benefits of their use.

## Effects Of MS

The lesions from MS can appear anywhere in your CNS and affect any part of your body.

Mobility issues

As you age, some disabilities from MS may become more pronounced. If you have mobility issues, falling may put you at an increased risk of bone fractures. Having other conditions such as arthritis and osteoporosis can complicate matters.

Other issues

One of the most common symptoms of MS is fatigue, but it's not uncommon for people with MS to also have:

- depression

- anxiety

- some degree of cognitive impairment

## Prognosis For People With MS

It's almost impossible to predict how MS will progress in any one person. About 10 to 15 percent of people with MS have only rare attacks and minimal disability ten years after diagnosis. This is sometimes called benign MS. About half of people with MS use a cane or other form of assistance 15 years after receiving an MS diagnosis. At 20 years, about 60 percent are still ambulatory and less than 15 percent need care for their basic needs.

## MS type

Progressive MS generally advances faster than RRMS. People with RRMS can be in remission for many years. A lack of disability after five years is usually a good indicator for the future.

## Age and sex

The disease generally progresses faster in men than in women. It may also progress faster in those who receive a diagnosis after age 40 and in those who have a high relapse rate.

# Natural Remedies And MS

Some herbs, supplements, and alternative therapies can cause:

• drug interactions

• adverse health conditions

• medical complications when used incorrectly

Ayurvedic Medicine For MS

Ashwagandha

This Ayurvedic herb is known by many names, including:

- Withania somnifera

- Indian ginseng

- Asana

Its berries, roots, and extracts are sometimes used for:

- chronic pain

- fatigue

- inflammation

- stress relief

- anxiety

Although some research into how ashwagandha can protect the brain has been promising, it's not been studied well enough to know whether it can effectively treat multiple sclerosis or its symptoms.

Barberry

Barberry, or Berberis vulgaris, has long been used in Indian and Chinese medicine for:

- easing inflammation

- fighting infection

- treating diarrhea

- calming heartburn

It can be used in many forms and may be used to boost the immune system. However, there's some evidence it doesn't interact well with certain drugs, so consult your healthcare provider first.

Chyawanprash

Chyawanprash is an herbal tonic commonly used in Ayurvedic medicine. Early animal studies indicate it may protect cognitive function by aiding memory. Formal studies on humans are scarce. There's not enough evidence to determine whether Chyawanprash is effective or helpful in managing MS symptoms.

## Chinese Herbs For MS
Astragalus

Astragalus is an herb that has been used for centuries in traditional Chinese medicine (TCM). Although there are many species of this plant, only two are typically used for medicinal purposes: Astragalus membranaceus and

Astragalus mongholicus. According to the National Center for Complementary and Integrative Health (NCCIH), astragalus is safe for most adults but may interact with drugs that affect the immune system. This herb is thought to affect the immune system, liver, and heart, but there hasn't been enough research in humans to fully understand its effects.

Burdock root

Arctium lappa, commonly known as burdock, has been used in traditional Chinese medicine (TCM) and European medicine for centuries. It's touted for its apparent ability to promote circulation and reduce inflammation. Burdock is being studied for its antioxidant and anti-inflammatory abilities, and its potential effect on cancer, diabetes, skin conditions, and the gastrointestinal system. Severe allergic reactions to burdock are possible. Not enough research on MS and burdock has been done to determine whether it's beneficial for people with MS.

Gotu Kola

Gotu kola is a popular traditional medicine in Chinese and Ayurvedic history. It's been promoted as an herb that can lengthen life and improve symptoms of eye diseases, swelling, inflammation, skin conditions, and fatigue. While some research has shown promise, gotu kola has been studied very little. Its actual impact on MS symptoms is unknown. It's available in a wide variety of forms, and it's generally considered safe in low doses.

Ginkgo Biloba

Renowned for its potential to improve memory and mental clarity, ginkgo has been used for a wide variety of ailments over the centuries. According to the NCCIH, ginkgo extract or supplements are possibly effective for:

• improving thinking and memory difficulties

• relieving leg pain and overactive nerve responses

• impacting eye and vision problems

• reducing dizziness and vertigo

It hasn't been widely studied in individuals with MS, but may help people living with MS by reducing inflammation and fatigue. Most people can safely take ginkgo in supplement form, but it may interact with a wide variety of other medications and herbs. For this reason, it's important to ask your healthcare provider before beginning the use of this supplement.

Huo ma ren (Chinese hemp seed)

This traditional Chinese medicine, used for its sedative properties for a variety of illnesses, is believed to soothe problems of the nervous system. Extracts from plants in the cannabis family have been studied for their role in reducing spasticity, neurodegeneration, and inflammation. Some practitioners believe that closely monitored use of specific members of this plant family can be highly effective for treating symptoms of MS, but its use in the clinical setting remains controversial.

Myrrh

Myrrh has historically been treasured for its aroma and use in ritual religious ceremonies. In addition, it's been used for centuries for its medicinal properties. It's believed to have antiseptic abilities and the power to treat diabetes, circulation problems, and rheumatism. It also appears to have beneficial anti-inflammatory properties for the modern treatment of health problems. It doesn't appear to have been studied specifically for symptoms of MS.

Herbs For MS

Agrimony

Current use of agrimony is based on centuries of its use in treating a variety of health problems. Although different medicinal properties are attributed to the many different varieties of agrimony, recent research has discovered antiviral, antioxidative, anti-inflammatory, and metabolism-boosting properties. Human research on this herb as a treatment for MS is virtually nonexistent, although some promising animal model studies are investigating the herb's properties as they relate to MS symptoms.

Bilberry leaf

Bilberry, also known as huckleberry, is a relative of the blueberry and can be used for its fruit or leaves. Although it's often used in foods, the berries and leaves can be used to derive plant extracts for supplements and other medicinal uses. Historically, this herb was used to treat everything from vision problems and scurvy to diarrhea and circulation problems. There are few reliable human trials studying this plant, and bilberry research specifically related to MS is virtually nonexistent. However, there's evidence suggesting bilberry is rich in antioxidants and has the potential to:

- improve vision

- reduce inflammation

- protect cognitive function

Catnip

Apparently, catnip is not just for kitties. Some individuals use this herb for MS pain management. However, catnip may actually make fatigue worse or multiply the effect of other sedative medications. Research in humans is lacking, but early animal trials on extracts of various species of this plant indicate that catnip may have anti-inflammatory abilities.

Chamomile

Chamomile has been used for centuries both topically and orally for:

- skin conditions

- sleeplessness or anxiety

- stomach upset

- gas or diarrhea

Trials in humans are few and far between, but its common use and availability in a variety of forms make chamomile a popular remedy for some people with MS. Chamomile offers antioxidant and antibacterial effects, and it's also being studied for its ability to prevent tumor growth and mouth ulcers in people with cancer. However, not enough is known specifically about chamomile's role in treating MS to indicate whether it's effective for this purpose.

Dandelion root and leaf

Korean medicine has used the dandelion in herbal remedies for energy improvement and general health, while Native American and Arabic medicine has used dandelion for digestive and skin problems. Animal trials suggest dandelion may reduce fatigue and promote immune health. Research also suggests that dandelion has antioxidant and anti-inflammatory effects. No research has examined the impact of dandelion on multiple sclerosis, but the plant does appear to have some medicinal properties that might be helpful to individuals with MS symptoms.

Echinacea

Echinacea is available in many forms and has long been used to treat colds and upper respiratory infections. Evidence is mixed as to its ability to prevent and treat colds. For people living with MS, research generally supports the plant's anti-inflammatory potential for the CNS. Some people may be allergic to echinacea and should take great caution with its use, but the herb is typically safe as a temporary supplement.

Elderflower

Elderflower is known by many names, including:

- European elder

- Sambucus nigra

- Elderberry

The berries and flowers of the elder tree have traditionally been used for:

- skin conditions

- infections

- colds

- fevers

- pain

- swelling

The uncooked or unripe berries are toxic, and inappropriate use of the plant can cause diarrhea and vomiting. Limited research supports the use of the elderflower in treating the flu and chronic inflammatory conditions. Animal studies also suggest elderflower extracts play a role in regulating immune response in the CNS. More research in humans needs to be done to define the potential of elderflower in managing MS symptoms.

Cramp bark

Cramp bark, or Viburnum opulus, is plant bark that's used to treat cramps and spasms. Although human research on this herb is in its infancy, it appears to have antioxidants and anticancer effects that may inhibit the growth of tumors or lesions.

Ginger

Ginger has long been used for its remarkable flavor and its medicinal purposes. In folk medicines, it's commonly used to aid in:

- stomach problems

- nausea

- joint and muscle pain

- diarrhea

Research is starting to uncover anti-inflammatory and neuroprotective potential in ginger and other spices. The potential role of ginger in preventing inflammatory problems makes ginger an excellent choice. Most people can tolerate reasonable use of ginger with few or no side effects.

Ginseng

There are several varieties of ginseng used for medicinal purposes. Most forms of ginseng have some well supported health benefits. Panax ginseng, for instance, is possibly effective for improving thinking and memory and relieving erectile dysfunction, although its safety is less well known. American ginseng may help prevent respiratory infections, and Siberian ginseng may have antiviral properties that could help fight a cold. Most forms of ginseng has shown benefits for people with diabetes, but all forms carry the risk of allergy and drug interaction. Always ask your healthcare provider before adding ginseng to an MS dietary regimen.

Hawthorn Berry

Hawthorn plants have long been used in medical treatments for heart failure or irregular heartbeats. More recently, it's been studied (primarily in animals) for its effect on circulation. Recent research also suggests it has antitumor and anti-inflammatory properties that could play a role in treating other diseases. In general, this plant has not been well studied for its effects on human health.

Licorice

Licorice root and its extracts have long been used to treat:

• viral conditions

• stomach ulcers

• throat problems

Very limited research suggests that licorice may reduce inflammation. It may also have some neuroprotective effects. Research is still insufficient to make a recommendation for the use of licorice to treat MS symptoms.

Milk thistle

Traditionally used as a liver tonic, milk thistle is being studied in the modern age for its impact on liver inflammation and health. The herb is available in a variety of forms (e.g., tinctures and supplements), but the appropriate dosage for treatment of conditions in humans is unknown. More research needs to be done before this herb can be officially recommended for treatment of MS symptoms.

Oat seed or oat straw

Whole oats are often used to reduce cholesterol and promote cardiovascular health. Despite their reputation for improving heart health, the research supporting oats' antioxidant and anti-inflammatory effects in humans is limited. Oat seed is believed to have antifungal properties. Oat straw is believed to be helpful for:

- MS

- spasms

- depression
- degenerative diseases

Peppermint

Peppermint has long been used topically and in the form of tea or capsules to:

- promote digestive health
- treat muscle and nerve pain
- relieve headaches
- ease nausea or stress

There is insufficient research to determine whether peppermint is clinically helpful for the treatment of MS, but research is promising for its effect on irritable bowel syndrome (IBS).

Red clover

Red clover is a legume that's historically been used to treat:

- respiratory problems
- cancers

- symptoms of menopause

Some research suggests it could help prevent cardiovascular disease, but long-term use of red clover may not be safe. It hasn't been evaluated in human trials for its impact on MS symptoms.

Sage

Throughout the ages, sage has been used for more than just its rich herb flavor. Historically, it's been used to address mouth and throat problems, indigestion, and mental acuity. While sage may have properties that are linked to memory enhancement and improved mood, there's not enough research in humans to know how effective it might be in treating MS symptoms.

Schizandra berry

Schizandra (Schisandra) berry is thought to have antiseptic and anti-inflammatory properties. Animal trials suggest it may also have a neuroprotective ability. However, schizandra berries have not been well studied for their potential to relieve MS symptoms in humans.

St. John's wort

St. John's wort has traditionally been used for nerve pain and mental health conditions, such as depression and anxiety, and as a balm for wounds. Its effect on depressive symptoms has been well studied. St. John's wort is starting to be evaluated for its ability to promote the healing and health of nerves. There's not enough research on St. John's wort and MS to be able to recommend its use for treatment of MS symptoms, but it may help with depression and inflammation. It may interact with a wide variety of medications and should be discussed with a healthcare provider prior to use.

Stevia

This popular alternative to sugar has long been used for diabetes treatment. Recent research has also identified antioxidant effects and other properties that could potentially improve liver and kidney health. There's not enough research on stevia and MS to be able to recommend its use for treatment of MS symptoms.

Turmeric

Turmeric is a popular spice containing curcuminoids. Curcuminoids have been shown to have neuroprotective effects. Its anti-inflammatory abilities also show promise for the alleviation of MS symptoms. However, its true impact on MS symptoms, and its proper dosage, must be studied further before it can be widely recommended for use by people with MS.

## Valerian

Traditionally used for headaches, trembling, and a variety of sleep disorders, valerian has also been used for anxiety and depression. Research on the effectiveness of valerian for insomnia and anxiety is mixed, but it may help with sleep problems. It's uncertain whether valerian is beneficial for effectively treating symptoms of MS.

## Wood Betony

Wood betony, or Stachys lavandulifolia, has traditionally been used as a tea to treat respiratory and digestive problems. Wood betony oil has antimicrobial and antioxidant properties. More research is needed to understand whether wood betony may be helpful in treating MS symptoms.

## Vitamins For MS

Vitamin A

This fat-soluble vitamin plays a critical role in:

- vision health

- reproductive health

- immune system health

Vitamin A is also important for proper function of the heart and other organs. Vitamin A can be found naturally in a variety of foods, such as leafy greens, organ meats, fruits, and dairy products, or obtained through a supplement. It's possible to overdose on vitamin A. It shouldn't be taken in large doses without the advice of a healthcare provider. Vitamin A supplementation has been linked to delays in age-related macular degeneration. The antioxidants in vitamin A may be helpful for people with MS, but the connection between vitamin A and MS hasn't been well explored.

Vitamin B-1 (thiamine)

Vitamin B-1, also known as thiamine or thiamin, is critical for proper brain function. Thiamine is also essential for healthy metabolism and nerve, muscle, and heart function.

Deficiencies in thiamine are associated with a variety of neurodegenerative conditions, including MS. Too little vitamin B-1 can also cause weakness and fatigue. Thiamine can be found in:

• nuts

• seeds

• legumes

• whole grains

• eggs

• lean meats

Vitamin B-6

Vitamin B-6 is an essential nutrient for metabolism that's found in certain foods, such as organ meats, fish, and starchy vegetables, and supplements. Although deficiencies are rare, low vitamin B-6 levels can occur in people with autoimmune disorders. Vitamin B-6 deficiency can be associated with:

• abnormal brain function

• depression

- confusion

- kidney problems

Research on B-6 and multiple sclerosis is limited. There's little scientific support indicating vitamin B-6 supplementation can prevent MS symptoms. Vitamin B-6 can be toxic to nerves if taken at too high of a dosage.

Vitamin B-12

Vitamin B-12 is important for the proper function of:

- nerve cells

- red blood cells

- the brain

- many other body parts

Deficiencies lead to:

- weakness

- weight loss

- numbness and tingling in hands and feet

- balance problems

- confusion

- memory problems

- even nerve damage

People with MS may be more likely to develop a B-12 deficiency, making supplementation a good option for some individuals. Together, vitamins B-6 and B-12 may be important for eye health. However, there isn't enough evidence to connect vitamin B-12 supplementation to improved MS symptoms.

Vitamin C

Vitamin C, or ascorbic acid, plays an important role in the function of the immune system. It's an antioxidant that people with MS may have trouble absorbing. Although vitamin C deficiencies are rare, they can cause serious problems, such as:

- depression

- tooth loss

- fatigue

- joint pain

- death

Some research indicates that ascorbic acid is essential to eye health and the prevention of macular degeneration and cataracts. Some early research suggests that vitamin C's antioxidants may help protect individuals with MS from nerve deterioration, but more research is needed.

Vitamin D

Vitamin D is essential for bone, muscle, nerve, and immune system health. Most people obtain vitamin D from:

- sun exposure

- fatty fish

- fortified foods and drinks

Research continues to suggest that there's a strong connection between vitamin D levels and the development and progression of MS. Sun exposure and monitored vitamin D supplementation is becoming a more common recommendation for the treatment of MS. However, more research is necessary before the practice becomes standardized and the strength of vitamin D's effects on MS is fully understood.

Vitamin E

Vitamin E is an important fat-soluble nutrient and antioxidant. It's essential for immune system health and preventing blood clots. Vegetable oils, nuts, and green vegetables are the best food sources of vitamin E. The antioxidant abilities of vitamin E have been of interest to researchers, and people with MS may already have low levels of vitamin E. However, there's not enough research on vitamin E and MS to know whether it's a truly effective treatment option for MS symptoms.

## Supplements For MS
Bee pollen or venom

Venom of honeybees, also known as apitoxin, is a clear liquid. Treatment of health conditions with the venom of bee stings is called apitherapy. Unlike many of the other herbs and supplements used to treat MS and its symptoms, bee venom has been specifically studied for its effects on MS in several clinical trials. These human trials were typically small. There's still not enough available research to know for sure whether venom-derived treatments may be beneficial for treating MS or they introduce negative health effects. Bee pollen, on the other hand, is increasingly used as a dietary supplement. Although its properties are still under investigation, it appears to have antioxidant and antimicrobial abilities, according to a 2013 study. A 2015 study showed that it's helpful in boosting immune system health and fighting chronic conditions. Research is limited, and people with suspected allergies to bee stings or bee pollen should avoid all treatment options using extracts or products from honeybees.

Calcium

Calcium is a crucial mineral for the body's health and proper function. It's a common part of many diets and is a common supplement. Research indicates that calcium plays an important role in:

• bone health

• cardiovascular health

• cancer risk

Proper levels of calcium are important for everyone, but individuals with MS who are also taking vitamin D or medications with one of these ingredients should consult their healthcare provider before adding one of these supplements to their routine. Vitamin D increases the body's absorption of calcium, and an overdose of calcium can be toxic.

Cranberry

Although cranberry juice (unsweetened 100 percent juice, not cocktail or mixed juices) and cranberry tablets have long been used to fend off urinary tract infections, research indicates that its benefit may be less than previously expected. However, diluted pure cranberry juice, which is high in antioxidants, and cranberry tablets may be an easy way to give people living with MS who experience bladder dysfunction a slight advantage. Complications with this remedy are rare.

DHA

DHA is an omega-3 fatty acid, docosahexaenoic acid, which can be obtained by consuming:

- vegetable oils

- fatty fish

- omega-3 dietary supplements

According to the National Center for Complementary and Integrative Health (NCCIH), DHA is essential for:

• blood flow

• muscle activity

• digestion

• cell growth

• brain function

In those living with MS, DHA supplements may help protect the CNS. Its ability to promote brain health may prove beneficial for people with MS. Side effects of DHA supplementation are typically mild, although it can thin the blood and make clotting difficult. Most people with MS may be able to safely use DHA supplements with their healthcare provider's oversight.

Fish or cod liver oil

Fish liver oil and cod liver oil are not the same as plain fish oils, which many people take for the omega-3 fatty acids. Liver oils from fish contain omega-3 fatty acids as well as vitamins A and D, which can cause overdose effects in large amounts. Some research indicates that cod liver oil is not as helpful as regular fish in the diet. It's important to note that the vitamin D in cod liver oil may have a protective effect prior to the onset of MS. In general, however, vitamin D and the fatty acids found in fish liver and its oils may offer a variety of health benefits from which people with MS aren't excluded.

Magnesium

Magnesium is essential for a wide variety of bodily functions. Deficiencies in this mineral can cause:

- weakness

- fatigue

- tingling

- cramps

- seizures

- muscle contraction

- numbness

- personality changes

Magnesium supplements and a diet containing natural sources of magnesium may be beneficial for preventing a deficiency that could aggravate symptoms of MS.

Mineral oil

Often used to treat constipation and for skin care, mineral oil is commonly found in cosmetics and laxatives. According to the National Multiple Sclerosis Society, the use of mineral oil for laxative purposes shouldn't be done for long-term relief. It's possible to overdose on mineral oil. Its minerals and vitamins can build up to toxic levels in the body. This oil can also make other gastrointestinal problems worse in some individuals.

Multimineral and multivitamin supplements

Although they can be purchased as separate supplements, many supplements combine numerous vitamins and minerals in a single pill or powder. In most cases, it's preferable to obtain as many nutrients as possible from a healthy balanced diet. However, some health conditions make it harder for people to get enough vitamins and minerals out of food, which makes it easier to develop deficiencies. There's still disagreement in the scientific community as to the importance of multiminerals or multivitamins in the prevention of a wide range of health conditions and the maintenance of health. Some evidence does suggest that certain varieties of multimineral and/or multivitamin supplementation may help prevent:

- brain inflammation

- neurodegenerative problems

- fatigue and cognitive problems

- other health problems

For some individuals with MS, a general multimineral-multivitamin supplement may help prevent deficiencies that could worsen symptoms of the disease.

Omega-3 and omega-6 essential fatty acids

Omega-3 and omega-6 are essential fatty acids (EFAs), or polyunsaturated fatty acids (PUFAs), that are revered for their potential to promote everything from a healthy cardiovascular system to a healthy brain. Although their exact impact on MS is yet unknown, clinical studies are underway. The anti-inflammatory and immune-promoting effects of these fats are expected to be a promising option.

These fatty acids can be found naturally in foods as well as in over-the-counter supplements.

Polyunsaturated fatty acids (PUFAs)

Polyunsaturated fatty acids (PUFAs) can be obtained naturally through your diet or in OTC supplements. Omega-3 and omega-6 fatty acids may be helpful for reducing inflammation and promoting health in a variety of ways, but the role of PUFAs in treating MS symptoms isn't well studied. Some research suggests that PUFA supplements may reduce the severity and length of MS relapses.

Probiotics

Probiotics are bacteria that are thought to be helpful to the body. They are often called "good bacteria" and are similar to the microorganisms found in the human body. Probiotics are available in the form of supplements and yogurts. In general, probiotics may have anti-inflammatory properties that may boost immune and neurological health.

Selenium

Selenium is a mineral that's becoming increasingly well understood for its contribution to human health. It has long been used to prevent heart problems and a number of different cancers, although scientific support for selenium's effects is limited. Research indicates it plays an important role in:

- eye health

- immune system health

- a variety of chronic health conditions

Soy lecithin

Soy lecithin is found in soybeans. It's rich in choline, which may be linked to better heart and brain health. It's not been studied well enough in people with MS to determine whether it's helpful for treating MS symptoms.

Zinc

Zinc is a mineral that's necessary in small amounts for human health. It's used to:

- boost the immune system

- treat a variety of eye problems

- address skin conditions

- protect against viruses and neurodegenerative conditions

More research is needed, but it's possible that some individuals with MS may benefit from the apparent promotion of eye health and the neuroprotective effect of zinc. Vitamins for MS

Made in the USA
Coppell, TX
09 September 2024

36973244R00046